HISTORY in a HURRY

Vikings

written and drawn by
JOHN FARMAN

MACMILLAN
CHILDREN'S BOOKS

First published 1997 by Macmillan Children's Books
a division of Macmillan Publishers Limited
25 Eccleston Place, London SW1W 9NF
and Basingstoke

Associated companies throughout the world

ISBN 0 330 35254 7

Text and illustrations copyright © John Farman 1997

The right of John Farman to be identified as the
author of this work has been asserted by him in accordance with the
Copyright, Designs and Patents Act 1988.

3 5 7 9 8 6 4

A CIP catalogue record for this book is available from
the British Library.

Printed and bound in Great Britain
by Mackays of Chatham plc, Kent

☁ CONTENTS

☞ OFF WE GO!

The poor old Vikings have always had a terrible press. Horrid, cross barbarians with red beards and nasty dispositions, criss-crossing the known world, raping and pillaging everyone who got in their way – that's what we always think of them. Good for newspaper sales but was that the full picture? The 'Viking Age', in all its forms, didn't actually go on for very long – AD 793 to AD 1066 to be precise – and they became better known for trading than raiding and dealing than stealing.

Where did They Come From?
It's tempting to think that one day a gang of red-headed heathens got together and decided to look for trouble, calling themselves Vikings, a bit like Hell's Angels (Bikings?). Instead of crash helmets they chose pointy tin hats with horns on. As a point of interest (maybe) most serious historians say that they never had horns on their helmets, but I've seen an ancient Swedish picture that says different, so – as it's my book – they're going to! Instead of mean motorbikes, the Vikings chose horses, or those long pointed-at-both-ends boats called . . . er . . . boats*. It must be said, however, that most of the world's population at that time (who *weren't* Vikings) did think them a frightfully rough, tough and dead common bunch. Except, of course, all those that stayed at home (womenfolk and farmers), who reckoned they were the bees' knees: young gladiators whose hair-raising escapades were followed with admiration by young and old alike.

*Dragon Ships actually. Ed

Who's for History?

But Vikingism didn't happen overnight. It was the result of centuries of Scandinavian history (Scandinavia's a smart word for Sweden, Denmark, Norway and Iceland). Unfortunately you'll have to take my word for this, unless you'd *prefer* a long, somewhat boring book on Scandinavian history*. All I will say is that 'the Ice Age put paid to anyone who happened to be scratching a living in Scandinavia around 24,000 BC and that the first chilly hunter-gatherers thawed out, and tiptoed back in 15,000 BC. They became Neolithic farmers around 3500 BC and stayed like that until the Viking Age began around AD 800' – and you can't get briefer than that!

OPTIONAL EXTRAS

STANDARD VIKING

PS If you notice annoying scribbles by someone called Ed in this book, I'm sorry, but it's Susie, my fussy editor. She's just doing her job, and the daft printer left them in by mistake and we didn't have time to change things before printing the book.

*Instead of a short, somewhat boring book? Ed

Chapter 1

HOW IT ALL HAPPENED: THE VIKING AGE FROM START TO FINISH

beat the Vikings at last. Allows them to stay up north but hangs on to the south.

885–886	Siege of Paris.
900	Harold I kicks off the great Norwegian Kingdom.
935–945	King Gorm the Old.
985	Eric the Red finds Greenland. Svein Forkbeard Christianizes Norway.
992	Leif Eriksson trips over America.
1017	Naughty old Forkbeard takes bribe money given to him by Ethelred the Unready (the English king) to go away, and uses it to pay a bigger army to attack Britain with.
1019	Foundation of the empire of Canute the Great.
1066	Harold is made king.

Good news: he defeats the Norwegians at Stamford Bridge.

Bad news: he loses to William the Conqueror (head Norman) at Hastings.

End of the Vikings.

Chapter 2

🐉 GLORIOUS GODS

According to legend, Vikings proper began with a swashbuckling chieftain called Odin, who led an Asiatic tribe to Scandinavia. His people gave him god-like status: Odin the All-Father, god of war and the occult, god of kings and Lord of the Slain . . . not to mention god of poetry and wisdom (which I'd have thought was quite enough to be going on with). Odin finally set up home in a place called Asgard which I reckon would have been somewhere in what we now call the Soviet Union (except we don't even call it that any more – or do we?*).

There he'd lounge upon his throne, in the palace of Valhalla, a huge hall with 640 doors, while his two helpers, Hugin (mind) and Munin (memory), sat on his shoulders surveying the universe.** Actually, Odin needed them rather badly as he'd apparently hung himself for nine days *and* given up one eye in his constant search for knowledge and magic wisdom. (I've given up my brain.)

Valhalla was, by all accounts, really groovy and Odin made it open house for dead warriors. To show his gratitude he ran a free taxi-horse service for anyone who happened to be lying dead on the battlefield, in the form of his personal eight-legged steed, Sleipnir. This super-horse would fetch them back to Odin's place, where they were met at the front door by beautiful maidens called Valkyries with gallons of beer and

*No. It's the Commonwealth of Independent States. Ed
**Shouldn't you mention they were ravens? Ed

EIGHT LEG
DRIVE

limitless salt and vinegar crisps (not really). They were then informed that they could spend the rest of their lives* doing what they liked best; having orgies, eating till they felt sick, drinking out of the skulls of their enemies and knocking eight bells out of each other (luckily they were already dead so they didn't have much to lose).

Valkyries

These were very much the sort of girls you needed around. They were the well-gorgeous warrior handmaidens of Odin and known as 'the choosers of the slain'. As myth would have it, they went to the battlefields and picked out the dead that had been on Odin's side – and ate the ones that weren't (see Viking Food).

* Shouldn't that be deaths? Ed

Good God Thor

The god the Vikings liked best, however, was Odin's eldest lad
– Thor the Thunderer, god of the sky, Lord Protector of the
Universe and the overall Chap in Charge of lightning, thunder-
claps and all that sort of stuff. He rode around the heavens in
a flash chariot pulled by two billy goats (names unknown)
easily recognized by red hair, red beard and red eyes (Thor –
not the goats). He was always waving his favourite hammer
(called Mjollmir) in case he came up against any of the giants
who had set up home beyond the limits of civilization
(Norwich?).

Useless Fact No. 42
It turns out that later Thor pinched all the giants' beer which
annoyed them no end (I can imagine just how they felt).

Frey'd So

The other god worth a few lines was Sweden's head god, Frey.
Frey was the god of fertility (very Swedish), and was always
recognizable by his constantly erect private part (and who
wouldn't be?)*, probably because he was obsessed with a
giantess called Gerd who lived in the underworld and whom
he eventually married. Frey was in charge of rain and sunshine
and was generally prayed to if a good time was required. (No
comment!) He owned a fab magic boat called Skioblaonir
which was so huge that it could carry all the
gods of Asgard, but still folded up into a
little pouch when it wasn't needed
(sounds like one of those silly bikes).

*Do we have to go into this? Ed

Other Good Gods' Names to Drop

🪶 Baldre: son of Odin and wife Frigg (see Unfortunate Names for Lady Gods). His main claim to fame seems to be being shot to death by his blind brother, Hod, who fired a sprig of mistletoe at him (beats all that sissy kissing-under business).

🪶 Ull: (a much better shot), brilliant at archery, god of hunting, and a champion skier (downhill slalom?).

🪶 Mimi: god of wisdom (and French singers?).

🪶 Loki: half god/half devil (a touch awkward?). He was a son of a giant and, being a big lad himself, married a lady giant (as you do). They had three rather odd kids – one a serpent, one a wolf and one, thank God, an actual godlet called Æsir. As if that wasn't enough, Loki personally gave birth to Odin's eight-legged horse (which must have given the midwife quite a turn). None of the other gods thought much of him, especially when he set up the aforementioned blind kid, Hod, to kill his brother Baldre. To get out of the ensuing fuss, Loki turned himself into a salmon (a touch fishy, methinks)*, but his own boy Æsir tied him to a rock on which a poisonous serpent was sitting. I think a little family counselling might have been in order – don't you?

*Please! Ed

Downsides of being a Viking God

One's long-term prospects left a lot to be desired. All the gods knew that one day they would all die in 'The Last Battle' when the world would be overtaken by the forces of chaos (which accounts for everything).

Chapter 3

TRADE . . .
§—VIKING STYLE

As was suggested in the first chapter, the Vikings, when not a-conquering, were mostly a-wheeling and a-dealing. In the winter, everywhere up Scandinavia way was as cold as a witch's . . . nose. All the major towns and cities were connected by wide tracts of slippery ice and snow. There was simply no point in inventing cars or trains, so they relied on sleds, skis, skates and tin-trays*.

Beloved Boats

For travelling further afield and for general use in the summer when the ice melted, the early Vikings preferred floating. Their very first vessels didn't have sails as, having taken rather a long time to discover the joys of the keel (the bit of wood that goes underneath), the long narrow boats had a tendency to go bottom-up if they tried to erect a mast. The sort of thing we now like to think of as proper Viking ships (the ones they went to war in) didn't really arrive until later.

The Vikings had a strange relationship with their boats,

*Are you sure about the tin-trays? Ed

almost like love affairs. For months on end these floating mobile homes would be their transport and their . . . um . . . homes.

Bigger Boats

The boats that the Vikings went trading in were much bigger than the little narrow fighting ships. These massive, broad vessels (called *knorr*) were anything up to 30 metres long, with open holds for cargo. As you can imagine, they were impossible to row, so carried vast sails (and vast keels presumably).

Useless Fact No. 69

For centuries after, any Danish woman with a larger than average bust was labelled knorr-breasted.*

Swapsies

The Vikings' main exports were: skins and furs, which were all the rage throughout the courts of Europe (no central heating involved); ivory from the tusks of walruses, either

*How very interesting. Ed

worked into jewellery or not (they ate the
rest); feathers of the eider duck
for duvets (they ate the rest of
them too); and amber
(fossilized pine-tree
juice) from the
Baltic region. They
also bred and trained
big birds (falcons) with
which the European
nobility loved to hunt
little birds. Best of
all, the Vikings had
a habit of capturing
anyone they happened across on
their travels, some (particularly the pretty girls) for home
consumption and some (the ugly ones) to trade on as slaves.

Useless Fact No. 83

Talking of slaves, the Vikings were the first people to pick up black
prisoners from North Africa who they called the 'blue men'.
Actually I'm not surprised they were blue, as it was reported that
the poor devils were constantly freezing when they got most of
them back to Scandinavia or Ireland. The rest they sold to Arab
merchants who were beginning to get everywhere.

The first Scandinavians to trade were the Swedes and the
Gotlanders (a Baltic island regarded as the centre of the Viking
Empire). They were mostly after hard cash (well, gold),
woollens and glass (which they weren't very good at) from
Europe.

Byzantium Bound

If you've ever heard of Byzantium, forget it, because it became Constantinople. If you've heard of Constantinople, forget that as well: it's now Istanbul. The Vikings went there when it was Constantinople – the greatest city in the world. It was their very favourite place and they visited in their thousands, just to drink in the history and, of course, to trade – there was loads of money there, and that's what the Vikings wanted most of all.

Chapter 4

🌬 *A-PLUNDERING WE WILL GO*

The trouble with empires is that they have a habit of declining and falling, and the Roman one was no exception. When it finally happened in AD 500, the whole of the West became exposed to any Tom, Dick or Svein that cared to invade. Britain, in a right state of disarray after the Romans had gone home (and being surrounded by water), was an obvious choice for the Vikings to practise on.

The first we Britons knew of the proper Vikings was in 793 when a nasty bunch of savages came roaring over from Norway and wrecked and plundered the monastery at Lindisfarne on the east coast of England. As monks weren't (and probably still aren't) that good at fighting, monastery-plundering turned out to be rather easy, so they came back the next summer (a kind of working holiday?). Having got the hang of it, they kept it up on and off for nigh on two and a half centuries, which was very boring if you happened to live here at the time (especially if you were a monk).

OH NO! NOT RAPE AND PILLAGE AGAIN

The raiders usually came on a Sunday, which was rather clever, as they knew that most people would be at church. The little-ish visits were really only a dress rehearsal for the big stuff which was to come later.

Space Alert

Meanwhile, the Scandinavian people were becoming fitter and stronger every day, due to a better climate, heavier harvests and therefore more grub. All this, coupled with the Scandinavian man's preference for having as many wives as poss (and old folk not dying so quick) caused the population to explode around AD 800 – so they *had* to start looking around for more land.

Free Trade

As soon as they started getting out and about a bit more, the more aggressive young Norsemen couldn't help noticing all the riches that were whizzing around the known world*, and, naturally, they wanted their share. Not having much in the way of hard cash, they only had two options – either to give the merchants things in return (called trade) or simply take what they liked (called robbing). No contest! Viking piracy was born.

Scottish McVikings

By the 9th century a few of the Viking warriors had set up home in Scotland, particularly in the outer islands. These were perfectly positioned for little shopping trips to England, France and Ireland where they would nick all the gold, silver, bonny sheep and bonny women they could find.

*They could hardly have worried about the unknown world. Ed

Irish O'Vikings

In 839 a whole gaggle of Norwegian Viking boats turned up at the north of Ireland and quickly conquered Ulster before heading down to find Dublin . . . which wasn't there so they founded it. Their leader, a rather rough gentleman called Thorgisl, promptly made himself King (as one did), but almost immediately boatfuls of dangerous Danish Vikings arrived to fight him for the ireland of Island* and the fickle Irish helped them. Actually the Irish had hated the first lot so much that they'd have welcomed practically anyone else.

Time for a Barbie

The first few battles were savage, the Danes making literally mincemeat out of the Norwegians. It made no difference in the end. Those darn Norwegians eventually got the upper hand

*I think you might have that wrong. Ed

and formed a mini-Empire consisting of Ireland, the Isle of Man and the west of England and it took a hundred years to get 'em out. The guy that got rid of them was an Irish king called Brian Boru (a king called Brian?), but by that time many of the Vikings had given up their horrid ways and decided to be nice Christians anyway.

Useless (and Distasteful) Fact No. 101

There's a gruesome report which tells of the victorious Danes cooking their supper on top of the piles of their dead enemies. As they roasted their meat amongst the corpses the heat caused the bellies of the dead men to burst, revealing last night's supper. I don't know about you, but I think that might just have taken an edge off my appetite.

Chapter 5

THE DEEPLY
DANGEROUS DANES

It might surprise you to know that the Normans who kicked the stuffing out of us in 1066 turned out to be ex-Vikings. How? Read on please.

Before the aforementioned 839 invasions of England and Ireland, the Danish Vikings had been keeping themselves busy elsewhere. By 834 they had become a touch bored with routine small-time rape and pillage and started to go in for conquering in earnest.

They began by attacking Friesland (Holland) and its top trading centre, Dorestad, which hung on by its fingernails for ten years until the sea, in the form of huge tidal waves, washed it away completely. Next, the Danes sent a fleet up the River Elbe to give Hamburg (now in Germany) a hammering and another up the Seine with a view to punishing Paris.

Luckily (for the Vikings), the whole Frankish Empire split in three in 843, weakening it no end. The Danish lot were now joined by the Norwegian lot, who'd been waiting in the wings (or harbours) ready to pounce. Poor old Charles-the-Bald, king of the French bit, must have lost most of his hair when they started attacking his lands (by 878 they had taken the whole lot

– right up to Paris). Paris was supposed to have been defended by the heir of Charlemagne (the boss of the whole empire), Charles-the-Fat, but was left with only 200 extremely nervous knights. Imagine the state of their trousers when they saw seven hundred strange ships rowing towards them containing 30,000 very vicious Vikings. It was a walkover, and in the end Charles (the-Now-Totally-Bald) had to pacify them with bucketfuls of Danegeld (the term used for all payments gratefully received by the Vikings).

Confused?

If you're getting in a bit of a pickle over which Vikings were which, and who actually plundered northern Europe, don't worry – they were all at it.

Time for a Rollo

The new leader of this all-conquering Viking force was an ex-pirate called Rollo, who was either a Dane, a Swede or a Norwegian (nobody's quite sure).

Useless Fact No. 127
Whatever he was, Rollo was, by all accounts, an absolute giant – too big for any horse to stand under him.

He'd been taking it easy up in Northern France but managed to do a smart deal in 911 with poor old Charles-the-

Bald (and-Now-Dead)'s successor – the aptly named Charles-the-Simple. I dread to think what we might call our Charles if and when he becomes king. Most of the good names have gone. How's about Charles-the-Ears?*

. . . anyway, the deal was to make Rollo ruler of Normandy in return for protecting it from attacks from Rollo's other Viking mates. Nice one!

Really Rollo!
Apparently, once any agreement was made, it was the habit to kiss the king's foot (unlike the more usual part of the anatomy!!)**. Rollo was so huge that he promptly bent down and lifted poor King Simple's foot to his mouth sending him flat on his back. All the other Vikings, not known for a highly-tuned sense of humour, fell on their backs as well – in uncontrollable mirth.

Once in the driving seat, Rollo encouraged his men to marry the rather pretty Frankish girls. Despite being asked nicely to become Christian, those naughty Vikings took Rollo's words literally and, remembering their old ways, took several wives each. A hundred and fifty years later, this new Frankish/Viking colony started peering cheekily across the channel at England. Read on!

Meanwhile, Back in England
As I've said before, the Danish didn't go in for small raiding parties, and took over the harassment of England from the Norwegians. It became so regular that some of them didn't even bother to go home between raids, staying in Britain over

*Please get on with it. Ed
**I hope you mean the hand. Ed

the winter. In 865 a 'Great Heathen Host' (Danish) led by, would you believe, brothers Halfdown-of-the-Wide-Embrace, Ubbi, and Ivar-the-Boneless (who, I imagine, was carried), arrived and set up home in East Anglia. They were the sons of Ragnor Hairy-Trousers*.

Useless Fact No. 144
Ragnor Hairy-Trousers was so called because of a special pair of double thick fur trousers, boiled in tar and rolled in sand as protection against dragon breath.

The Great Alfred the Great
The Danes built forts all along the Thames and used them as bases to attack the rest of our, at that time, Anglo-Saxon land. They were joined in 871 by the 'Great Summer Army' and together they attacked Wessex (the last independent kingdom in England). Alfred, King of Wessex, though rather poor at cakes, was rather good at fighting and did his best to stop them, but although he managed to re-grab most of what the Danes had taken, Alfred carelessly died in 899, letting them conquer us back. It was thanks to him, however, that Britain never became a completely Viking land.

By the tenth century the Danes had taken just about everything from North Yorkshire down to the Thames (including Watford) and we were nearly all Vikings again. Actually, they should have spent a little more time looking in their rear-view mirrors, as in the meantime, Denmark been taken over by Olaf (who I think was a king) for Sweden.

By 927, however, we had our own brave new king called Edward (Alfred's eldest lad) who, with his sister Aethelflaed,

*You're making this up, Mr Farman. Ed
Look, don't blame me, I got this from Magnus Magnusson's (him of Mastermind) fab book on Vikings. JF

gave the new Viking leaders (Danish) such a hard time that they were forced to join us, the English, to fight – here we go again – the Norwegians. Honestly, it must have been hell to live in England in those days – you wouldn't have known whether you were coming or going*. Things were peaceful for fifty years until those pesky Vikings started up again. A certain Svein Forkbeard (son of the late, great Harald Blue-Tooth, who'd made Denmark a Viking nation) tried to attack London, and was given 16,000 pounds of silver to stop pestering us (cheap at twice the price). The Danes were to become famous for their pay-us-or-we-won't-go-away approach to diplomacy (and war).

SVEIN FORKBEARD

MONEY FOR ENGLAND

Ready or Not

By 1002, Ethelred the Unready (our new English king) had had enough of Scandinavians and ordered every Dane on British soil to be killed (even his own Danish soldiers). Extreme but rather effective. This upset Svein, now the new Danish king, considerably (as his little sister was one of them) and he came over to conquer us yet again – talk about pass-the-

*I certainly don't! Ed

parcel. This time he was paid 36,000 pounds of silver to get lost (that's inflation for you). His successor, the great grandson of the aptly named Gorm the Old, King Canute (him of damp feet fame) finished the job. We were now officially conquered. So did we all become Vikings again? Of course not. Canute's sons were useless at ruling and by 1035 the Danes had practically disappeared – yet again.

So there we have it. Britain, having just got rid of all its own Vikings, was now ready and set to be invaded by the Normans under William the Conqueror, who were simply relatively recently *ex*-Vikings. That's life, I suppose.

Harold's Bad Day

The king of England at the time was a chap called Harold Godwinesson (sounds like an insurance salesman). He'd got a call to tell him that another Harold (or rather Harald, to be strictly correct) had just arrived up north with a load of Norwegians in a fleet of three hundred ships and was marching down (without the ships) towards York. Harold promptly marched his army up the M1* and took them by surprise at Stamford Bridge, killing Harald-the-Ruthless (and-Now-Lifeless) in the process. Harald's son, on pain of severe tickling, promised faithfully to never try it again.

Harold and his army were just sitting down for a well-earned cuppa when a messenger rushed in and told him that William had just landed in – you've guessed – the south of England; Hastings to be precise. William hadn't been able to believe his luck, as there hadn't been so much as an angry dog to stop them, let alone a Saxon Dads' Army. Poor Harold then had to rush his already well-knackered army to meet them, but

*Don't be ridiculous. Ed

was shot in the eye* and badly killed at the Battle of Hastings on 14th October 1066.

Useless Fact No. 160

The final blow came three years later when a sad group of Viking Warriors, who'd presumably missed the last boat home, were massacred by William the Conqueror's men.

But the Viking Age, as such,
was as good as over.

*No he wasn't. That's just folklore. Ed

Chapter 6

THE NAUGHTY NORWEGIANS

The Norwegian Vikings never quite knew where to stop where conquering was concerned. Not content with the British Isles and France, they pushed further afield, crashing into Southern Spain, and on to Portugal and even North Africa.

Iceland Ahoy

Their biggest migration, however, was to Iceland. Ten thousand of them sailed and skidded their way across, promptly getting rid of the few Irish settlers who'd been scratching a meagre living there for ages. The climate wasn't too different to home, so it was a doddle for the Vikings to farm and rear animals. They became what was known as – you'll never guess – 'Icelanders' and soon set up trade connections with the continent, dealing in skins and furs. Having loads of wives certainly did wonders for the population, so it wasn't surprising that in less than a hundred years they'd multiplied over six times. Sadly, Iceland soon showed all the tell-tale signs that it couldn't support a huge population (and we all know what that feels like). Things got so bad, in the end, that they were reduced to throwing the old and helpless over cliffs to keep the population down (I hope this doesn't give our government any ideas). It was time to get those boats out again . . .

Eric the Red

In 982, one of their bravest men, called Eric the Red, was kicked out of the country for three years for being very naughty (mass murder or something). I suppose he didn't have a lot going for him, having bright red hair, being deported *and* being called Eric. (If there are any red-haired Erics out there . . . sorry.) Feeling somewhat rejected, he decided to go somewhere that nobody else had – so struck out west. After a lot of hard rowing he and his chums came across a completely new land. Well, to be absolutely honest, it wasn't really land, just ice. But once he'd got past all the white ice-floes and bergs, Eric stumbled upon a huge bit that was positively green. Obviously he couldn't go back straightaway (on pain of instant head removal), so waited a couple more years before trolling back to Iceland to tell everyone that he'd found a country that, in a moment of divine inspiration, he'd called Greenland.

GREAT MOMENTS IN EXPLORATION

The following year, 25 boats set out with all that was needed – animals, women, cheese and pickle sandwiches, etc.* – to set up a brand new colony. The one thing that Eric had forgotten to tell them, however, was that Greenland had hardly any trees. Normally, this wouldn't have been a problem, but the Vikings used wood for everything from cooking to building houses and novelty pipe-racks. Consequently, they soon got a bit fed up with this new country.

Look with Leif

In 992 Eric's boy, Leif Ericsson (Eric's son – geddit?), whose main hobby had been making everyone Christian, became equally fed up with everyone moaning about the country his dad had found. So Leif set off with 35 mates to find somewhere else (which they did). 'Else' turned out to be the coast of Labrador (named after a dog)** which was not too welcoming (no shops), so they pushed on south to a really fab place with more trees than you could shake a . . . er . . . stick at, which they named Vinland ('cos they found grape vines there). The only slight problem were large bands of what they unkindly labelled 'ugly men', who turned out to be Red Indians (and who later turned into politically correct Native Americans). Now, you don't get a degree in geography for sussing where they'd arrived. You got it! They'd just stumbled onto the set of a Western.*** Sorry – they'd discovered America (so all that stuff about Christopher Columbus discovering it five centuries later, which you might have read in one of my other books, is probably pure baloney).

Just as the cowboys were to find out years later, those pesky redskins were rather tricksy to deal with on a friendly basis,

*I don't think so somehow. Ed
**I think you'll find the dog just might have been named after the land. Ed
***Pleeeease! Ed

and far too tough on an unfriendly basis (and can you blame 'em?). So, because Leif and his followers couldn't ring home for back-up (and to cut a long story very short) they packed up their boats and hurried back to Greenland, forgetting all about the New World.

Useless Fact No. 172

Following the Vikings' daft habit of shoving a descriptive label on everyone, Mr Ericsson had been labelled Leif the Lucky (which I think was a touch premature as things turned out).

LEIF THE (UN)LUCKY

Chapter 7

AT HOME WITH
MR AND MRS VIKING

One of the downsides of having your husband away most of the time raping and pillaging, was that women had to do all the things that the men would do had they been there (which they weren't). Consequently, women became very good at running the small farms that were dotted throughout Scandinavia. Rich and powerful men often had several women (nothing's changed there then) but there was always one *proper* wife.

Marriage Money
Not only would her husband-to-be pay her a tidy sum, but her dad would also have paid a dowry when the young man took her off his hands, which I think is a splendid idea. If the marriage didn't work out, pa would get his cash back (and presumably his daughter as well).

Society Wedding
Like many societies of the time the new husband would be led to his bride by a group of witnesses who would wait around to see them at it just to make sure the whole business was consummated (look it up!). Unlike these days, the wife would keep her own name, but if some sort of row broke out between

her new husband and her old family, she could choose which side she wanted to be on. Divorce, rather surprisingly, was easy and these were some of the 'acceptable grounds':

1. The wearing of trousers by a woman (rather unreasonable).

2. Impotence. If the  husband couldn't fufil his marital duties (reasonable).

3. The wearing of girlish clothes by a man (extremely reasonable).

4. Friendliness towards anyone who had killed one of your partner's family (about as reasonable as you can get).

Once a Slave . . .

Owing to the high incidence of concubines and slaves, there were usually a lot of extra-marital kids hanging around. Unfortunately, if you were a slave girl's child you could expect to be a slave all your life. This was the law, but in practice, if a slave was well-liked he could become one of the family in most senses of the word, even down to being adopted by the boss. If a child wasn't favoured he or she might face being thrown into the sea to save expense, which seems quite a neat solution to over-population if you ask me.*

How to Stage an Adoption – Viking Style (in six easy steps)
1. Slaughter a three-year-old ox.
2. Invite all available friends and family to your house.
3. Make a boot from the hide off the ox's right leg** (the rest to be eaten at feast).
4. Set boot in middle of room.
5. Make everyone at the party put their right foot in this new boot, including the adoptee. (This makes him or her one of the family.)
6. Presumably scout around for the left leg to make up the pair (and another ox, if you've eaten the last one).

What's for Lunch?
Nothing, is the short answer. There would be two meals a day: the first (*dagveror*) was at eight or nine in the morning, after a couple of hours' work, and the second (*nattveror*) in the early evening. Both meals would be similar.

There might be cheese, followed by the odd dried raw herring smeared with butter, or Coco Pops if you preferred***. Also on the menu there might be porridge and a kind of gruel made from leftovers with lots of rough bread (Viking's Pride?). Drink-wise, they went in for a yukky kind of beer called mead which was made from fermented honey.

In the evening they'd mostly eat meat (preferably boiled) – anything from cows to horses to bears to whales to reindeer –

*We didn't. Ed
**Front or back? Ed. You choose. JF
***I'm losing patience. Ed

all garnished with lots of onions and cabbage. When they ran out of those they were forced to eat seaweed . . . of which there was lots. Having more ice and salt around than they could possibly use, meant that the Vikings were not too concerned about food preservation (so they didn't use their fridges much).*

Eating In

As restaurants hadn't been invented yet, the Vikings ate in quite a lot. They cooked over big fires in the middle of the kitchen-cum-dining-cum-bed-cum-sitting- (Come Dancing?) room. This was usually a long hall with raised platforms down each side, on which they all sat. Well, all except the master and mistress, who would sit in the middle on carved 'thrones' facing the central hearth.

The Vikings ate off wooden plates using spoons and knives (no forks yet) and drank out of drinking horns (the ones that weren't stuck on their hats).

After supper, they'd sit in the smoky room (no chimneys) talking and telling rude jokes, while the womenfolk did handy things with their hands. When it was bedtime the servants brought in mattresses stuffed with hay and a load of sheepskins for the cold night ahead.

*I've lost it. Ed

Family Fun

Obviously, everyone sleeping in one room causes a certain lack of privacy (if you get my meaning). This never worried the Vikings – they just got on with it as they pleased. Imagine if your parents did all that after dinner in your house.

Cleanliness

Most people think of the Scandinavians as being rather clean people (positively squeaky I think). Some were and some weren't in Viking times. There's no doubt that the Swedes weren't. They didn't clean themselves after going to the loo and didn't wash their faces before going to bed. They did, however, have a daily routine that went something like this.

Early in the morning your servant girl would bring a large bowl of water to your head man. He'd then wash his hands and face and comb his hair over the bowl. Then he'd blow his nose and spit into the water.

Unconventional but OK so far. When he was done, however, the girl took the same bowl to the person next to him, who repeated the process. By the time it got to the last person, everyone had blown their noses, combed their hair and spat into the water. Lovely.

The Danes, on the other hand, used to wash their faces (and behind their ears), comb their hair, and even take the odd bath on Saturday nights – in *different* water. I know which *I'd* choose for a weekend guest!

Useless Fact No. 181

However clean or unclean, all Vikings had a nasty habit of washing their clothes in cow pee (yes, cow pee!) while waiting for the discovery of soap.

At the Doctor's

For a start, there weren't any. They did, however, have ways of treating severe stomach wounds – of which they had many. Here's what they did.

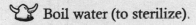 Boil water (to sterilize).

Dress the wound.

Make patient swallow a special porridge made of onions and herbs.

If a subsequent smell of onions came from the wound, it meant that his intestines had been pierced and that he'd soon be a goner anyway.

Either way, I bet his breath left a lot to be desired.

Useless Fact No. 182

The Viking poet Thormod Kolbrunarskald, after having an arrow wrenched from his heart, and on being offered the porridge, was heard to remark, 'Take it away [I bet they weren't his actual words], I am not suffering from the porridge illness', which meant that the wound was not in his stomach but in his chest.

Medicine Men

Although the Swedish Vikings didn't have doctors as such, they did have medicine men (*attiba*). But don't be fooled. These were more like wizards, so your average poorly Viking, having made an appointment to go to his 'surgery', would simply be told what to sacrifice to which gods to make his problem go away. Simple illnesses would demand some animal or other but, if it was a little more serious (flu?), he'd demand a human sacrifice (some slave or naughty child) which he'd hang on a pole outside his house until the sacrifice was dead from exposure. Certainly beats a couple of aspirin and a day in bed.

Chapter 8

JUST THE THING: LAW AND ORDER

When you can't think of anything appropriate to call something, you sometimes refer to it as a 'thing'. This obviously happened when the Vikings tried to think of a name for their assemblies. "Are you going to the er . . . *Thing* tonight?" they must have cried.

Anyway, after a while the name must have stuck and each district would have its own Thing in order to decide and administer the law and all the stuff that crops up when a lot of people live together. Free men of good standing in the community would meet to put the law, which had been memorized and passed down through the generations by word of mouth, into action and discuss the really important local issues like who stole Sven Bigbelly's best pig, or who ran off with Harald Bluebottom's missus.

There were little THINGS and big THINGS. The big THINGS met only twice a year and the elders of the society sorted out the problems that the little THINGS couldn't.

Things varied from Viking country to Viking country, but we know they had them when they colonized England which at that time was divided into *wapentakes* (the area covered by the attending members). Are you getting bored with Things? I am. Let's move on to some more gory bits.

Punishments

As we saw from their 'be-murdered-or-pay-up' type of blackmail, the Vikings were very much into money and nearly all crimes could be settled by payments (*mannboetrr*). If you killed someone or chopped off his nose you could expect the full fine.

If you simply poked his eye out you'd probably get away with half that amount, and for a simple ear lop – half again.

The judgement was made by the THING*, but catch this. They thought that *any* crime was against society (bad parking?), so the fine had to be paid whatever. If there was a feud between a very rich, very powerful family and a very poor, very weak one, the poor devil from the weaker side, who'd had whatever done to him (the victim!) was made to pay the compensation. I don't know about you, but from where I'm sitting this all seems a trifle unfair. I imagine that historians, in all their wisdom, would see this as a major flaw in the Viking legal system.

Strangely enough, stealing was regarded as the worst crime of all and the thief could expect a severe hanging – not out of some moral outrage, but because they presumed the culprit would be poor (why else would he steal?) and thus wouldn't be able to pay the fine anyway.

If a dispute became boring, because it was too difficult to

*Oh no, not THINGS again. Ed

sort out, it would either be sent to the big THING or the two parties involved would be made to fight a duel to the death – which seemed to satisfy everybody (even the loser).

DEAD HAPPY

Chapter 9

WHO WAS WHO?

One tends to think that once you've seen one Viking you've seen 'em all. But like us now, they had a rigid class structure. The best breakdown of all the different classes I can find comes from the famous Icelandic poem called *Rigspula* (song of Rig). But reading Scandinavian poems is like watching paint dry, so I'll just give you the drift of it.

The Thralls

Right at the bottom of the pile were the *Thrall*. These were the poor folk, captured and brought over from England, Scotland and Ireland, who weren't sold to the Arabs. Their status left a lot to be desired; you can see this by the names they were given. The lower than low serf boys (serfers?) were given descriptive surnames like Foolish, Grumpy, Clot, Ugly or just plain Fat, and the poor girls, Clumsy, Fat Legs, Big Nose or Talkative (sounds like my old school).

Being a Thrall was no fun at all, since Thralls were totally bound to their master and had no freedom or status. Blimey, you could even kill a Thrall and get off with not much more than a wagging finger.

On the plus side, although they had to slog their guts out on the land during the day, after work (providing they could still stand) many could do what they liked. If they managed to earn money, it was not uncommon for a Thrall to buy himself back off his master, thus achieving his freedom.

EXCUSE ME, YOUR LORDSHIP, HOW MUCH AM I?

Great, isn't it? Not only do you get stolen, but then you've got to use your own money to buy yourself back.

The Peasants

These were a different matter and were highly regarded in Viking society. They were all smallholders or warriors and, most of all, free men with fab names like Brave, Smith, and Settler. The girls had somewhat dull names like Modest, Ornament, Quick or simply Woman. The best thing about being a Scandinavian Peasant during Viking times was that, unlike practically anywhere else at the time, they were free men. This meant that they didn't have to give up half their crops (or their best-looking daughters) to the local gentry every five minutes. Actually, the Viking Peasants were fab farmers, which is saying something when you consider that the land was colder than a vampire's handshake for most of the year. I won't go on about agriculture, however – we all know what farmers do.

The Earls

The Earls were the aristocracy who gave the poor old Thralls such a hard time. They included all the local chieftains and above them the rich land-owners. The Earls called their boy children smart names like Noble, Heir and Lineage or – if they were stuck for anything better – Son. Unfortunately, the aforementioned poem, *Song of Rig*, forgot to mention the girls' names but if you use your imagination, they could well have been Grace, Culture or Sharon.* At the top of this particular class was the King, who was chosen by the chiefs at the THING (King's Things?), but, when it came right down to it, the king couldn't really *do* anything without their permission. Having said that, some Kings were just boring old two-bit chieftains who liked the sound of a title, and who lorded it over a mere single valley or fjord.

Earls, on the other hand, were not to be messed with. Most had their own private armies made up of Peasants who, if having served their master well, could expect a golden handshake of either gold (literally) or land.

Here's a poem from a bloke at Harald Fairhair's Court, which gives the idea.

> *They are favoured with wealth and the*
>   *finest sword blades*
> *With metal from Hunland and maids*
>   *from the East;*
> *Glad they are when they guess*
>   *battle's near,*
> *Swift to leap up on the deck and lay*
>   *hands on the oars,*
> *To snap off the grommets (ouch!)*
>   *and splinter the tholes (OUCH!),*
> *And smite billows bravely at their*
>   *lord's bidding.*

Get the gist? Barking mad, the lot of 'em.

*I think not. Ed

Useless Fact No. 187

A Peasant's biggest buzz, apparently, was to get himself killed in battle right in front of his Lord (I'd have just pretended).

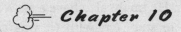 **Chapter 10**

VIKING WARRIORS

I said in the first chapter that not all Vikings were fighters, but it must be said that the ones that were... were good at it. It must also be remembered that as well as the ones that went on boat trips, there were lots of other types of Viking warriors. They had foot soldiers and cavalry as well.

The Infantry

Only the big, burly lads were used as foot soldiers. It was no job for wimps. They'd be kitted out with a chainmail vest, or an iron breastplate covered in leather.

Useless Fact No. 199

One nobleman was reported to have worn twelve coats of reindeer hide. Nice idea – it certainly kept the arrows out, but it was so heavy that I doubt whether the poor devil could walk.

On top of the Viking warrior's conical head he'd wear a conical (and somewhat comical) tin hat (horns optional), with a metal guard to save nose removal in battle. In his belt he'd have an assortment of deeply politically incorrect combat knives. In one hand he'd have a standard issue bow – often strung with his girlfriend's golden tresses (see Bald Warrior-Babes), and in another a sharp spear. He might also have a *sax* – not to get the enemy dancing, but to stab 'em with (it was a long single-edged sword). In another hand* he'd have a huge, round wooden shield with a metal bit in the middle. They're the ones you see stuck on the outside of Viking boats. Sometimes he'd put all that lot down on the grass and wade in with a whacking great, not-to-be-messed-with, long-handled battle-axe which could chop a man down the middle (shield, horse and all).

The Cavalry

Although most Vikings were great on horseback, best of all were the Magyars imported from Hungary. These guys were so flash that they could've got jobs in circuses (if there'd been any). They could fire an arrow at full tilt, chop a chap's head off with a swing of a sword, kebab three men in a row with a poke of a lance, and jump through fiery hoops if required – and that was *without* the horse!

Proper Vikings

I know, that previous stuff's all very well, but what about the Vikings that went out to sea in those funny boats? The Dragon Ships, full to the brim of vicious Vikings, were feared throughout the western world – and quite rightly.

Useless Fact No. 201

The Dragon Ships' very best design feature was that you didn't have to turn 'em round to make a quick get-away. No need for reverse gear – these boats were the same at each end. All the rowers had to do was swing round on their bottoms, quick as poss, and row like mad the other way.

*Three-armed Vikings eh? Ed

Berserkers

If you've ever heard the term 'going berserk', it might (or it might not) interest to you know that the expression came from a rather extreme bunch of Vikings called the *berserk* who suffered from a condition called *berserkganger* (a kind of battle fever). The word comes from 'bear shirt' or even 'bare-shirt', and it appears that these chaps went into battle with no armour and sometimes no clothes at all, save maybe a wolf's head stuck over theirs (head that is)*. They could, by all reports, turn themselves into vicious animals (hamsters?) at will, biting and tearing their enemies limb from limb with their bare hands and teeth, all the time leaping up and down and making funny howling noises (sounds like West Ham supporters). They were, as a group, in great demand and each King or Earl would try to have a bunch of them in his army.

*What else could they stick it over? Ed

Dead Good

If you were a Viking warrior, one of the most important things to remember was how to die with honour. Here's a description from Yuletide AD 980 when Harald Gormsson of Denmark tried to get his thoroughly drunk soldiers to crush his enemy, Earl Hakon of Norway.

They arrived at the battlefield sporting terrible hangovers and were promptly trounced. Their victorious enemy roped the surviving seventy warriors together and told them to wait patiently to be executed.

One by one the now extremely sober soldiers were released from the rope and calmly walked over to the execution block where they were quietly beheaded. The doomed men even played a sort of game which was to see who could hang on to his dagger the longest – after their head had dropped off (see Stupid Games in Ancient Times). One by one their daggers fell, the instant their heads left their necks. One, just to be different, asked to be chopped full in the face so that his mates (the ones who were still alive) could observe him not going pale. Okay, it killed him, but at least he didn't go pale.

Anyway, when it got to number eleven, an eighteen-year-old lad with beautiful long, blond hair stepped up. He asked politely if one of the executioners could possibly hold his hair away from the blade to avoid it getting covered in blood (vain or what?). The executioner obligingly wrapped the lad's hair round his hands and pulled it away from his head. As the axe was falling, the naughty lad, just for a laugh, whipped his head back causing the poor guy's arms to be lopped off at the elbows.

The Norwegians thought this was a great laugh and offered

the boy his life. He accepted, but only on condition that they
let the rest of his chums go free (with heads on),
which they did. Damned decent of
'em, I say.

Chapter 11

HORRIBLE THINGS §—*VIKINGS DID*

Ragnor's Great Balls-Up

By the mid 860's, Ragnor Hairy-Trousers (father of the lads Halfdown-of-the-Wide-Embrace, Ubbi, and Ivar-the-Boneless who led the Great Heathen Host, see p24) had grown jealous of his three sons' fame and decided to set sail for England to do a little conquering himself.

He was, unfortunately, a trifle past it, and was himself soon captured by King Aella of Northumbria. When he wouldn't say who he was, they threw him in a snake pit (all the rage in those days) to make him reconsider. Unfortunately, it didn't really work for, as the snakes were setting about him (poison and all), he started singing the Death Song of Ragnor, which instantly shot to the top of the charts.

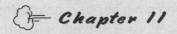

HOW THE PIGLETS WOULD GRUNT...

It ended with the immortal words
> *'How the piglets would grunt*
> *if they knew the plight of the boar.'*

Sounds bonkers, I admit. What have pigs got to do with anything? It turned out to be a reference to his three boys, who were indeed pretty miffed at the plight of their dad (the old boar).

The story goes that when top son Ivar-the-Boneless got his hands on the naughty King Aella, he managed to avenge the old man's death pretty darned well. He chose a tried and tested torture, and dedicated it to head god Odin.

First they carved a blood-eagle on the king's back (a popular pastime), and then hacked all the ribs from his spine. They then pulled the poor chap's lungs through the new hole in his back and spread them across his back to represent wings (more like water wings, I'd have thought*).

Worse to Come

Ragnor Hairy-Trousers' boys really got a taste for this sort of thing. There is a report in the Anglo-Saxon Chronicle (which, dear editor, was *not* a newspaper but a real live historical document) relating to the death of King Edmund of East Anglia in 870 or thereabouts: 'and they slew the king.' Not very inspiring, eh? But it later came out that Ragnor's three lads did it with considerably more style than they were given credit for. If you're not feeling in tip-top condition, I'd recommend that you take a break from Viking history at this point. It's not very nice.

As the saga goes, they tied poor Edmund face forward to a tree, and used him for bow and arrow practice. When he

*Sicko! Ed

resembled a hedgehog, and was no doubt feeling far from well, they pulled him off the tree and slit his back from top to bottom, exposing his complete ribcage. Just so that he didn't think he was getting off lightly, he was then split apart on the rack.

Useless Fact No. 215

The Anglo-Saxon Chronicle has it that at some point in the proceedings, Edmund's head went astray. His chums, lost in the forest while looking for it, called out to one another, 'Where are you?' They were surprised when Edmund's head answered, 'Here! Here!' Having tracked it down, they buried the head with his somewhat less-than-showroom-condition body.

When, years later, the coffin was exhumed (dug up again) the head and the body were found to be perfectly joined together – with just a wee scar, like a red silk thread.

Things You Must Do to Become a Saint

The good news was that Edmund was made a saint as compensation. All's well that ends well – see?

Getting them Back

Don't go thinking that it was only the Vikings who did horrid things. If one of the invaders got separated from the rest of the bunch, the Saxons had a rather unpleasant punishment, so legend has it. The poor unfortunate would be relieved of his skin whilst still alive, and said skin would be nailed to a monastery door. This 'Daneskin', as it was known, was supposed to serve as a warning to other invaders. All in all, I think I'd probably have got the message*.

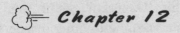

Chapter 12

RITUALS AND
BURIALS

The Swedish Vikings were particularly big on sacrifice. One of their favourite ones was held every nine years in Uppsala, Sweden, at which nine men and nine males of every type of available animal – dogs, horses, field-mice, etc. – were stabbed to death and hung up on trees in a sacred (and somewhat smelly) grove.

At one of their larger events, no less than seventy-two miscellaneous carcasses were observed by a Christian visitor (Holy Moses!).

Useless Fact No. 216

Vikings simply loved hanging people on trees and thought it rather a whizz to do it after battles. Failing that they'd chuck their conquests over cliffs
or into bogs.
Hey ho.

Going to the Blot?

Sacrificial feasts were called *blots*. If you wanted to join in, the only thing required was to bring beer to drink and dead horses to eat. The walls of the temple were decorated with the horse blood and the horse flesh was cooked for supper on the floor. The feast was dedicated to Odin, Njord, Frey and junior god Bragi.

The Passing of the Horse Willy

Here's another odd custom. In ancient Norway (before telly was invented) Mum, Dad, the children and their pet Thrall (slave) would sit of an evening, passing a horse's willy (horse unattached) wrapped in linen round and round, while reciting little verses. One night St Olaf and some mates were passing by and caught them at it. He thought this was far too pagan and rude* so he flung the horse's willy (called *volsi*) to the dog (name unknown) and proceeded to teach them Christianity – and about time too.

PASS THE WILLY, MOTHER

*Quite right. Ed

Burials were even weirder...

How to Conduct a Poor Man's Funeral

🐂 Make little boat and burn man in it.

How to Conduct a Chieftain's or Rich Man's Funeral (as happened on the river Volga in AD 922)

🐂 Take one freshly dead chieftain.

🐂 Bury him in a freshly dug grave for ten days while making his funeral costume.

🐂 Brew loads and loads of *nabid* (Viking beer) and get totally ratted for ten days.

🐂 Ask among female slaves and servants if anyone wants to die with him. (If no one volunteers – nominate someone.) Sometimes, if agreeable, his wife might do the job.

🐂 Wash volunteer's feet.

🐂 Bring dead man's ship to shore and place wooden bench covered in precious rugs and silks in it. Cover bench with tent.

🐂 Summon old hag (preferably a giant*), henceforth to be known as 'The Angel of Death'.

🐂 Dig up chieftain, now black from the intense cold, and dress him in new outfit.

🐂 Throw fruit and veg and all his old weapons in front of said stiff.

*Why? Ed

🛡️ Find stray dog, cut in two, and fling into ship.

🛡️ Take two horses (must be sweaty), cut into tiny pieces and chuck into ship also.

🛡️ Add two cows (also in little pieces) for flavour.

🛡️ Tell doomed slave girl (or wife) that she must make love to all the dead man's mates, to whom she must say 'I did this for him' (sounds reasonable).

🛡️ Take one chicken, remove head and throw rest into ship.

🛡️ Put girl/wife in tent next to ex-master/husband and send in six more men . . .

🛡️ Send Angel of Death into tent to wrap rope round girl/wife (handing the ends to men outside tent).

🪖 Angel of Death then proceeds to stab poor girl/wife while men pull as hard as poss on rope. Meantime ask everyone outside to bash their shields noisily.

🪖 Get naked friend to set light to ship making sure to keep one hand on his right buttock.*

🪖 Push boat out to sea and go home.

. . . and this, dear friends, is what we're dealing with.

*Enough! I'm sure you're making this up. Ed
Sadly not. JF

☁ TIME'S UP

That's it, folks! A fine bunch they turned out to be. If, after reading this lot, you feel that, contents-wise, this mighty work has been a little on the light side, may I remind you that you only paid half the price of a Happy Meal . . . and for that reason you should be grateful. I have to admit, however, there's been tons more written on the subject and I'd be the first to advise you to get down to your library (where it's free and you won't have to waste another half-Happy Meal) and get in amongst those naughty Vikings.

But if you've had quite enough of them, and I don't really blame you if you have, why not expand your massive brain with another book in this series? Please don't read too quickly, though; it takes me literally *hours* to write them.

Ready for another one? Here's just some of the fascinating information that we've snuck in to the book on . . .

Ancient Egypt

Useless Fact No. 381

Some Pharaohs had loos in their pyramid (in case they were caught short in the long afterlife).

The Downside of Having a Good Time in Ancient Egypt

1. No telly.

Downsides to Being a Pharaoh

⚠ Pharaohs were put through rigorous physical tests to prove they were superhuman. They often had to cheat.

⚠ Pharaohs had to get up in the dark every single morning. Otherwise the day wouldn't start and it would be their fault.

⚠ Women could be kings (occasionally) but not queens, which involved a certain amount of cross-dressing (false beards and stuff). Highly babish Cleopatra came much later – but was Greek, so didn't really count.

⚠ Being a god could be lonesome at times, as you were far too fabulous, wise and good for anyone else to talk to (I know the feeling*).

⚠ There was a set time for everything you did. Holding audiences, eating meals, giving judgements, going to the loo, having a bath, taking a walk, or even sleeping with the wives. Boring or what?

⚠ Because of all the dodgy interbreeding, the Pharaohs were often a bit dippy and sometimes barking mad.

Useless Fact No. 382

To get rid of mice, the Ancient Eygyptians smothered the house in fat made from boiled-up cats. (Presumably, to get rid of cats they smothered the house with fat from boiled-up dogs).

*And just who d'you think you're kidding? Ed